Big and Small

by Rod Theodorou and Carole Telford

Contents

RIGBY
INTERACTIVE
LIBRARY

© 1996 Rigby Education
Published by Rigby Interactive Library,
an imprint of Rigby Education,
division of Reed Elsevier, Inc.
500 Coventry Lane
Crystal Lake, IL 60014

Illustrations by Gwen Tourret and Trevor Dunton
Color reproduction by Track QSP
Printed in China

00 99 98 97 96
10 9 8 7 6 5 4 3 2 1

ISBN 1-57572-060-4

Library of Congress Cataloging-in-Publication Data
Theodorou, Rod.
  Big and small / by Rod Theodorou and Carole Telford;
[illustrations by Gwen Tourett and Trevor Dunton].
    p.   cm. — (Animal opposites)
  Includes index.
  Summary: Compares the habitat, feeding patterns, and behavior of the
elephant and ant, as determined by their physical attributes.
  ISBN 1-57572-060-4 (lib. bdg.)
  1. Animals—Juvenile literature. 2. Elephants—Juvenile literature.
3. Ants—Juvenile literature. 4. Body size—Juvenile literature.
[1. Elephants. 2. Ants.] I. Telford, Carole, 1961–
II. Tourett, Gwen, ill. III. Dunton, Trevor, ill. IV. Title.
V. Series: Theodorou, Rod. Animal opposites.
QL49.T34 1996
591.5—dc20   95–36315
                                                       CIP
                                                       AC

Photographic Acknowledgments
Babs and Bert Wells/OSF p5 *l*, back cover; Manis Wildlife Films/OSF p5 *r*; Hans Reinhard/Bruce Coleman p6 *l*; Martyn Colbeck/OSF pp6 *r*, 8, 14, 18 *b*, 20; Brian Rogers/Biofotos p7 *l*; Colin Milkins/OSF p7 *r*; C W Helliwell/OSF p9 *tl*; John Cooke/OSF p9 *bl*; J A L Cooke/OSF pp9 *r*, 15, 17, 19 *l*, 21; Ajay Desai/OSF p10; Neil Bromhall/OSF p11; Jeanne Drake/Tony Stone Images p12; K G Vock/Okapia/OSF p13; Rafi Ben-Shahar/OSF p16; Johan Elzenga/Tony Stone Worldwide p18 *t*; James H Robinson/OSF p19 *r*
Front cover: Dianne Blell Photography *l*; Michael Fogden/OSF *r*

brown bear

walrus

elephant

Some animals are big.
Some animals are small.

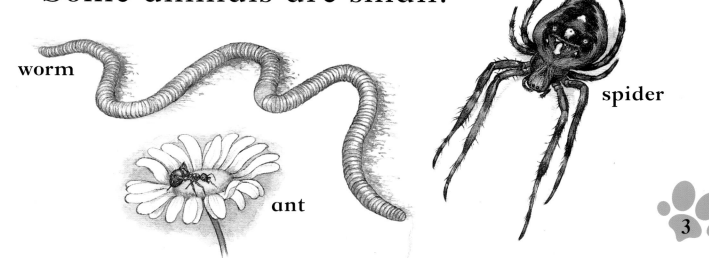

worm

ant

spider

These are
elephants.
Elephants
are very big
and slow.

This is an ant.
Ants are very small
and move quickly.

eye

jaw

5

There are
two kinds of
elephants.

Asian elephant

African elephant

They are
Asian elephants
and African
elephants.

6

There are many different
kinds of ants.
Ants live all over the world.

leaf-cutter ant

black ant

Elephants live together in herds.
The oldest cow elephant leads
the herd.

calf   cow

wood ant nest

Thousands of ants
live together in a nest.
Every nest has a
few big queen ants.

army
ant
queen

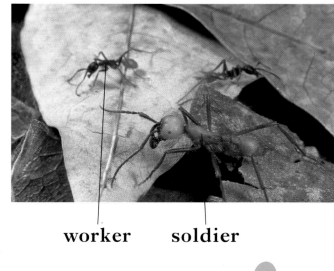
worker   soldier

Elephants are very strong.
An elephant can lift a heavy log.

Ants are strong, too.
This ant can carry a big
piece of plant.

Elephants eat a lot of plants and drink a lot of water.
An elephant drinks 25 buckets of water a day!

Some ants eat plants.
Most ants eat other creatures.

14

An elephant
can pull down
branches from
trees to eat
the leaves.

Ants work together to carry leaves back to their nest.

Elephants stick out their ears to make their heads look bigger. This frightens away their enemies.

Soldier ants fight off enemies.
They can bite or squirt acid.

Elephant
mothers
have one
baby every
three years.

18

Mothers feed
their babies
with milk
for four years.

Every year, a queen ant lays
thousands of eggs.
Worker ants look after the eggs.

queen leaf-cutter ant

Baby elephants love to play.

Ants never play.
They are always hard at work.

AMAZING FACTS!

An elephant's toenail is bigger than your hand.

Sometimes elephants make sunhats out of leafy branches.

There may be up
to half a million
ants in one nest!

Leaf-cutter ants
can strip a tree
bare in one night!

Index